JAM, JELLIES
pickles
preserves

JAMS, JELLIES
& pickles
preserves

making the most of seasonal vegetables, fruits and flowers

HELEN SUDELL

This edition published by Lorenz Books
an imprint of
Anness Publishing Limited
Hermes House
88–89 Blackfriars Road
London SE1 8HA

A CIP catalogue record is available from the British Library

ISBN 0-7548-0350-3

Publisher: Joanna Lorenz
Project Editor: Joanne Rippin
Designers: Lisa Tai and Lilian Lindblom

Previously published as part of the *Gifts From Nature* series

Printed and bound in Singapore

1 3 5 7 9 10 8 6 4 2

Acknowledgements: thanks to the following project contributors:
Stephanie Donaldson pp12, 13, 21, 30, 39, 44, 45, 48, 49, 56, 57, 59, 61, 62; Tessa Evelegh p47; Joanna Farrow p52;
Rafi Fernandez pp15, 16, 17; Gilly Love pp46, 60; Janice Murfitt pp32, 38, 42; Katherine Richmond pp20, 29, 33, 41;
Liz Trigg pp14, 18, 24, 26, 28, 34, 40, 58; Pamela Westland p31; Steven Wheeler p50.
Photographs by: Edward Allwright, James Duncan, John Freeman, Michelle Garrett, Nelson Hargreaves, Debbie Patterson.

CONTENTS

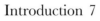

INTRODUCTION

*E*ven though you can now buy most varieties of fresh fruit and vegetables all year round, there is still nothing more satisfying than stocking the shelves of your store cupboard with your own home-made preserves. If you grow your own produce, there are lots of delicious ways to make the most of a bumper harvest. Vegetables and herbs can be turned into mouth-watering chutneys, or they can be kept in oil which will take on their flavour. Vegetables, fruit and herbs can be pickled in or used to flavour vinegar, while fruit, herbs and flowers can also be preserved in alcohol or turned into wines and liqueurs.

Home-made jams and jellies are the perfect way to deal with a glut of fruit and have an intensity of flavour rare in commercial varieties. Don't be put off by the thought of lengthy preparation. Some preserving sugars have added pectin, which means that the jam needs to be boiled for only a few minutes to reach setting point, retaining the fresh flavour and colour of the fruit. In fact, it is quite possible to make a pot or two of delicious jam in under half an hour.

Deft finishing touches will turn something everyday into something special and home-made pickles and preserves are a particular pleasure both to give and to receive. When you are making preserves intended as gifts, choose stylish bottles and jars, perhaps in decorative recycled glass, and tie or glue on labels handwritten with a flourish. The glowing colours of jams and jellies are beautiful in themselves but will be enhanced by pretty covers of fabric or paper, tied with raffia or ribbon.

Techniques and Containers

PRESERVING PRODUCE

To ensure that harmful bacteria are eliminated from fruit and vegetables bottled in brine, syrup or their own juices, you will need to sterilize the filled bottles before storing them. For this they must be heated thoroughly, either in a pan of water or in the oven. Always use clean, undamaged bottles with fresh rubber seals, and test the seal of every bottle. Bottles which have faulty seals should be used immediately and not stored for future use.

Sterilizing bottled preserves in a water bath

1 Use a special sterilizing pan or a large saucepan. Line the base of the pan with either a folded cloth or a wooden trivet.

2 Place the bottles, with their lids fastened, in the pan and fold a cloth around each one to prevent them touching.

3 Fill the pan with cold water to cover the bottles by a depth of at least 2.5 cm/1 in. Bring slowly to a simmer, then continue to simmer for the required time.

4 Once the sterilizing is complete and the bottles have cooled, check their seals by loosening the metal clips and making sure that the lids stay in place.

Sterilizing bottled preserves in the oven

Rest the lids on the bottles but do not seal. Stand them on a baking sheet lined with newspaper and place in a very low oven (120°C/250°F/Gas ½) until the contents are simmering well. Remove the bottles from the oven and seal immediately. As they cool, a vacuum will form inside to complete the seal and preserve the contents.

CHOOSING AND PREPARING CONTAINERS

Glass jars and bottles are best for most pickles and preserves. Glass is durable, versatile and easy to clean, and both reveals and enhances the appearance of its contents. Modern recycled glass is inexpensive and easily available, and its subtle colouring and texture give it an interesting antique look. Old-fashioned sweet jars, preserving jars and jam pots can be bought in junk shops and, providing that they can be properly cleaned, used to great effect. However, don't use them for any bottling that requires sterilizing.

Sterilizing jars

To sterilize jars in a dishwasher, use the hottest wash but without any detergent. If you do not own a dishwasher, wash the jars in hot, soapy water and rinse thoroughly. Stand them the right way up on a wooden board (making sure that they are not touching) and place the board in a cold oven. Turn the oven to very low (110°C/225°F/Gas ¼) and leave the jars for 30 minutes. If they are not to be used immediately, cover with a clean cloth.

Seals

The type of seal required depends on the preserving process used. For jams and jellies, providing the jars are thoroughly washed and dried before you use them, a circle of waxed paper and a paper cover are sufficient to keep the contents in good condition.

Seal jars of pickles and chutneys with plastic or plastic-coated metal screw tops: don't use paper covers as these allow the vinegar to evaporate, which will make the mixture shrink and become very dry within a few weeks.

Wines and liqueurs keep well in bottles sealed with new corks. Vinegars and oils can be sealed with either corks or screw tops, but bottled fruit and vegetables must be sealed with new rubber seals.

Labelling

Label your preserves with a description of the contents and the date they were made. You can use self-adhesive labels, but bear in mind that if you intend to store preserves in a cellar or larder where conditions can be slightly damp these may slip off, and it would be better to use tie-on labels. If your cellar is extremely damp, use something more durable, such as metal or wooden labels tied to the necks of the bottles or jars.

Storing

Keep pickles and preserves in a cool, dark place for up to a year, and use the contents of your store cupboard in rotation. Once jars have been opened, keep them in the fridge.

CHUTNEYS AND SAVOURY PRESERVES

*P*ickles and chutneys are easy and rewarding to make and are an excellent way to deal with a glut of fruit or vegetables. They add a delicious tang to bread and cheese or cold 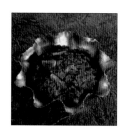 meats, and are always welcome as presents. Here there are some hot and spicy recipes from India, where chutneys have their origin, as well as more homely, traditional ideas for using unripe fruit from the garden.

 Vary the combinations of flavours to suit your own taste. The long, slow cooking results in a smooth texture and a mellow flavour which will be enhanced if the preserves are left to mature.

HARVEST CHUTNEYS

GREEN APPLE CHUTNEY

Almost every family has a few recipes for pickles and preserves that have been passed down from generation to generation. This one is wonderful with grilled sausages.

- 1 kg/2¼ lb green apples
- 15 g/½ oz garlic cloves
- 1 litre/1¾ pints/ 4 cups malt vinegar
- 450 g/1 lb dates
- 115 g/4 oz stem (preserved) ginger
- 450 g/1 lb/2½ cups seeded raisins
- 450 g/1 lb/2 cups brown sugar
- 2.5 ml/½ tsp cayenne pepper
- 25 g/1 oz/1 tbsp salt

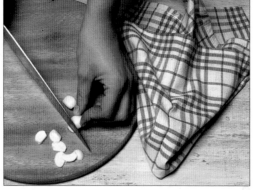

2 Peel and chop the garlic and place with the apple in a saucepan.

1 Quarter, core and chop the apples.

3 Pour in enough vinegar to cover and boil gently until soft. Chop the dates and ginger and add them to the cooked apple and garlic, together with all the other ingredients. Simmer gently for 45 minutes. Spoon the mixture into warmed, sterilized jars and seal immediately.

GREEN TOMATO CHUTNEY

Unripened tomatoes are a culinary success rather than a horticultural failure when transformed into a delicious chutney.

- 1 kg/2¼ lb green tomatoes
- 450 g/1 lb apples
- 2 medium-sized onions
- 1 litre/1¾ pints/ 4 cups malt vinegar
- 425 g/15 oz/2 cups brown sugar
- 250 g/9 oz/1⅓ cups
- sultanas (golden raisins)
- 7.5 ml/1½ tsp mustard powder
- 5 ml/1 tsp ground cinnamon
- 1.5 ml/¼ tsp ground cloves
- 1.5 ml/¼ tsp cayenne pepper

1 Quarter the tomatoes and place them in a large preserving pan. Quarter, core and chop the unpeeled apples and add them to the tomatoes. Chop the onions and add them to the tomatoes with all the other ingredients.
2 Heat gently, stirring, until all the sugar has dissolved. Bring to the boil and simmer, uncovered, stirring occasionally, for 1½ hours until the chutney has thickened.
3 Pour the chutney into warmed, sterilized jars and seal immediately.

WINDFALL PEAR CHUTNEY

*The seemingly unusable bullet-hard pears
that litter the ground beneath old pear trees
after a high wind respond beautifully
to cooking and can be used to make this
tasty chutney.*

- 675 g/1½ lb pears, peeled, cored and chopped
- 225 g/8 oz onions, chopped
- 175 g/6 oz/1 cup raisins
- 115 g/4 oz apples, cored and chopped
- 50 g/2 oz preserved stem ginger, chopped
- 115 g/4 oz/1 cup chopped walnuts
- 1 garlic clove, chopped
- juice and rind of 1 lemon
- 600 ml/1 pint/ 2½ cups cider vinegar
- 175 g/6 oz/¾ cup brown sugar
- 2 cloves
- 5 ml/1 tsp salt

1 Place the pears, onions, raisins, apples, ginger, walnuts, garlic, lemon juice and rind in a bowl.
2 Put the vinegar, sugar, cloves and salt into a saucepan. Heat gently, stirring, until the sugar has dissolved, then bring to the boil briefly and pour over the fruit. Cover and leave overnight.
3 In a preserving pan, boil the mixture gently for 1½ hours until soft and thickened. Spoon into warmed, sterilized jars and seal.

TOMATO AND RAISIN CHUTNEY

If you grow your own tomatoes, it's a pleasure to share them with your family and friends. This chutney is delicious with a selection of cheeses and crackers, or with cold meats.

- 900 g/2 lb tomatoes, skinned
- 225 g/8 oz/1⅓ cups raisins
- 225 g/8 oz onions, chopped
- 225 g/8 oz/1 cup sugar
- 600 ml/1 pint/2½ cups malt vinegar

1 Chop the tomatoes roughly. Put them into a preserving pan.

2 Add the raisins, chopped onions and sugar to the pan.

3 Pour over the vinegar. Bring to the boil and let the mixture simmer for 2 hours, uncovered. Spoon into warmed, sterilized jars and seal immediately.

SPICY TOMATO CHUTNEY

This delicious relish is especially suitable as an accompaniment to lentil dishes. It can be kept, covered, for up to a week in the fridge.

- 90 ml/6 tbsp vegetable oil
- 5 cm/2 in cinnamon stick
- 4 cloves
- 5 ml/1 tsp freshly-roasted cumin seeds
- 5 ml/1 tsp nigella seeds
- 4 bay leaves
- 5 ml/1 tsp mustard seeds, crushed
- 4 garlic cloves, crushed
- 5 cm/2 in piece fresh ginger, crushed
- 5 ml/1 tsp chilli powder
- 5 ml/1 tsp ground turmeric
- 60 ml/4 tbsp brown sugar
- 800 g/1¾ lb can chopped tomatoes, drained (reserving juice)

1 Heat the oil on a medium heat and fry the cinnamon, cloves, cumin and nigella seeds, bay leaves and mustard seeds for about 5 minutes. Add the garlic and fry until golden.

2 Add the ginger, chilli powder, turmeric, sugar and the reserved tomato juice. Simmer until reduced, add the tomatoes and cook for 15–20 minutes. Cool and serve.

INDIAN PICKLES AND CHUTNEY

HOT LIME PICKLE

A good lime pickle is not only delicious served with any Indian meal, but it also increases the appetite and aids digestion.

- 25 limes
- 225 g/8 oz/1 cup salt
- 60 ml/4 tbsp ground fenugreek
- 60 ml/4 tbsp mustard powder
- 60 ml/4 tbsp chilli powder
- 15 ml/1 tbsp ground turmeric
- 600 ml/1 pint/2½ cups mustard oil
- 5 ml/1 tsp ground asafoetida
- 30 ml/2 tbsp yellow mustard seeds, crushed

1 Cut each lime into 8 pieces. Place the limes in a large sterilized jar or bowl. Stir in the salt. Cover and leave in a warm place for 1–2 weeks, until the limes become soft and dull brown in colour. Blend together the fenugreek, mustard powder, chilli powder and turmeric and add the spice mixture to the limes. Cover again and leave in a warm place for a further 2–3 days.

2 Heat the mustard oil in a frying pan and fry the asafoetida and mustard seeds. When the oil reaches smoking point, pour it over the limes. Mix well, cover with a clean cloth and leave in a warm place for about a week before serving.

Main picture: top – Hot Lime Pickle, bottom – Green Chilli Pickle.

GREEN CHILLI PICKLE

*This really hot pickle from southern India is said to cool the body.
After bottling, leave it to mature for a week before serving.*

- 60 ml/4 tbsp yellow mustard seeds, crushed
- 60 ml/4 tbsp freshly ground cumin seeds
- 30 ml/2 tbsp ground turmeric
- 50 g/2 oz garlic cloves, crushed
- 150 ml/¼ pint/⅔ cup white vinegar

- 75 g/3 oz/⅓ cup sugar
- 10 ml/2 tsp salt
- 150 ml/¼ pint/⅔ cup mustard oil
- 20 small whole garlic cloves, peeled
- 450 g/1 lb small green chillies, halved

MANGO CHUTNEY

*This sweet chutney is usually served as an accompaniment to curries
but also makes a delicious addition to a cheese sandwich.*

- 50 ml/2 fl oz/¼ cup malt vinegar
- 2.5 ml/½ tsp dried chillies, crushed
- 6 cloves
- 6 black peppercorns
- 7.5 ml/1½ tsp onion seeds
- 175 g/6 oz/¾ cup sugar

- 450 g/1 lb unripe mango, peeled and cubed
- 5 cm/2 in piece fresh ginger, finely sliced
- 2 garlic cloves, crushed
- thinly cut rind of 1 orange or lemon (optional)
- salt, to taste

1 Mix the mustard seeds, cumin, turmeric, crushed garlic, vinegar, sugar and salt together. Cover and leave for 24 hours to allow the spices to infuse and the sugar and salt to dissolve.

2 Heat the mustard oil and gently fry the spice mixture for about 5 minutes. Add the whole garlic cloves and fry for a further 5 minutes.

3 Add the chillies and cook gently for about 30 minutes, until they are tender but still green. Cool thoroughly and pour into sterilized bottles, ensuring the oil is evenly distributed between the bottles.

1 Heat the vinegar with the chillies, cloves, peppercorns and onion seeds, salt and sugar. Simmer for about 15 minutes, until the vinegar is infused with the flavours of the spices.

2 Add the mango, ginger, garlic and citrus rind, if using. Simmer until the mango is mushy and the mixture well reduced. Cool, then pour into sterilized bottles. Leave for a few days before serving.

TRADITIONAL PICCALILLI

The piquancy of this bright yellow relish makes it an excellent partner for sausages, bacon and ham.

- 675 g/1½ lb cauliflower
- 450 g/1 lb small onions
- 350 g/12 oz French beans (green beans)
- 5 ml/1 tsp ground turmeric
- 5 ml/1 tsp mustard powder
- 10 ml/2 tsp cornflour (cornstarch)
- 600 ml/1 pint/ 2½ cups vinegar

1 Trim away the leaves and most of the stem of the cauliflower and cut the curd into tiny, evenly sized florets.

2 Peel the onions and top and tail the French beans (green beans), cutting them into shorter lengths if you wish.

3 Put the turmeric, mustard powder and cornflour (cornstarch) into a saucepan and add the vinegar. Stir well to blend the spices, bring to the boil and simmer for 10 minutes.

4 Put the prepared vegetables into a large pan and pour over the vinegar mixture. Mix well and simmer for 45 minutes. Pour into warmed, sterilized jars and seal immediately.

Farmhouse Pickles

Delicious traditional pickles such as these mean that seasonal produce can be enjoyed throughout the year.

DILL PICKLES

A glut of outdoor-grown ridge cucumbers can be turned into these piquant pickles to enjoy throughout the winter with hamburgers and cold meats.

- 675 g/1½ lb ridge cucumbers
- large bunch fresh dill
- 5 garlic cloves, peeled and sliced
- 900 ml/1½ pints/3¾ cups white wine vinegar
- 45 ml/3 tbsp coarse salt
- 6 black peppercorns
- 6 white peppercorns
- 2 bay leaves
- 1 star anise

1 Trim the ends off the cucumbers and cut them into 5 cm/2 in pieces. Place the pieces in a bowl of cold water, cover and refrigerate for 24 hours. Drain the cucumber and, using a wooden toothpick, pierce each piece in several places.

2 Pack the cucumbers into sterilized jars with the dill and garlic.

3 Pour the vinegar into a saucepan with 350 ml/12 fl oz/1½ cups water, then add the salt, peppercorns, bay leaves and star anise. If you prefer a sweeter pickle, add 45 ml/3 tbsp sugar to the vinegar mixture. Bring the mixture to the boil for 5 minutes, then pour over the cucumbers.

4 Seal immediately. Store for at least 2 weeks before eating.

PICKLED SHALLOTS

These shallots have a delicious sweet-sour flavour with none of the harshness that is sometimes associated with pickled onions. If the unpeeled shallots are softened in hot water, they are much easier to peel, and if you do this under water your eyes will be much less irritated.

- 675 g/1½ lb shallots
- 3 bay leaves (1 for each jar)
- 600 ml/1 pint/2½ cups malt vinegar
- 175 g/6 oz/¾ cup sugar
- 50 g/2 oz/¼ cup sea salt
- 10 ml/2 tsp pickling spice
- 7.5 ml/1½ tsp balsamic vinegar

1 Place the shallots in a large bowl and cover with boiling water. Leave for 10 minutes, then remove the shallots and peel them. Pack them into sterilized jars with one bay leaf in each jar.

2 In a saucepan, heat the malt vinegar with the sugar, salt and pickling spice. Stir until the sugar has dissolved completely, then bring to the boil. Remove from the heat and add the balsamic vinegar. Pour over the shallots and seal immediately. Store for 2 weeks before eating.

PICKLED PEARS

Pickled pears go well with country-cured ham and buttery mashed potatoes.

- 1 kg/2¼ lb hard pears
- juice of 2 lemons
- 675 g/1½ lb/3 cups brown sugar
- 1 litre/1¾ pints/4 cups cider vinegar
- 250 ml/8 fl oz/1 cup water
- 3 cinnamon sticks
- 3 star anise
- 5 ml/1 tsp black peppercorns
- 5 ml/1 tsp allspice berries

1 Peel the pears and toss them in the lemon juice to prevent discoloration. Place them in a large saucepan with the remaining ingredients and bring to the boil. Reduce the heat to a simmer and cook for about 45 minutes until the pears are nearly tender.

2 Spoon the pears with the syrup into sterilized jars. Seal immediately.

SWEET JELLIES AND JAMS

hese recipes range from traditional strawberry jam to delicate flower-scented preserves such as rose petal jelly. Apart from these summer flavours, there are ideas for preserves that can be made at any time of year and for aromatic jellies that make perfect accompaniments to roast meats. If you don't have a sugar thermometer, test for the setting point of a jam or jelly by spooning a little

of the hot mixture into a chilled saucer and leaving it to cool slightly. If setting point (105°C/221°F) has been reached, a skin will quickly form and will wrinkle when you push it with your finger.

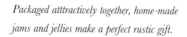

Packaged atttractively together, home-made jams and jellies make a perfect rustic gift.

STRAWBERRY JAM

This classic recipe is always popular. It's very important to leave strawberry jam to stand for a while before potting it and to stir the fruit into the jam so that it does not all end up at the tops of the jars.

- 1.5 kg/3 lb strawberries
- 1.5 kg/3 lb/6 cups sugar
- juice of ½ lemon

1 Wash and hull the strawberries and mash a few of them. Warm the sugar in a bowl in a low oven (120°C/250°F/Gas ½).

2 Put the mashed and whole strawberries into a preserving pan with the lemon juice and bring to a gentle simmer.

3 Add the warmed sugar and let it dissolve slowly over a gentle heat. Then let the jam boil rapidly for 10–15 minutes, or until setting point is reached. Remove from the heat.

4 Leave to stand, then stir until the strawberries are well distributed throughout the jam. Pot into warmed, sterilized jars and seal immediately.

THREE FRUIT MARMALADE

Home-made marmalade may be time-consuming to prepare, but the results are incomparably better than store-bought varieties. This tangy version can be made at any time of year.

- 350 g/12 oz oranges
- 350 g/12 oz lemons
- 700 g/1½ lb grapefruit
- 2.5 litres/4¼ pints/ 10¼ cups water
- 2.75 kg/6 lb/ 12 cups sugar

1 Scrub all the fruit thoroughly with a vegetable brush, and rinse. Use unwaxed fruit if you can find it.

2 Put the fruit into a preserving pan. Add the water, heat gently and simmer, uncovered, for about 2 hours.

3 When the fruit is very tender and the liquid has reduced to about half its original volume, remove the fruit and quarter it. Scrape out the pulp, extracting any pips, and return it to the pan with the cooking liquid.

4 Cut the rinds into slivers, and add to the pan. Add the sugar and heat gently until dissolved, then bring to the boil and cook until setting point is reached. Leave to stand for 1 hour, then pour into sterilized jars and seal immediately. Store in a cool, dark place.

LEMON AND LIME CURD

Limes add extra zest to this old-fashioned spread, which is wonderfully enlivening on toast or muffins. The curd will keep, unopened, for up to a month. Once opened, keep it in the fridge and consume within a week.

- 115 g/4 oz/½ cup unsalted (sweet) butter
- 3 eggs
- grated rind and juice of

- 2 lemons
- grated rind and juice of 2 limes
- 225 g/8 oz/1 cup caster (superfine) sugar

1 Place the butter in a bowl set over a large pan of simmering water. Lightly beat the eggs and add them to the butter. Add the lemon and lime rinds and juices.

2 Add the sugar and stir the mixture constantly until it thickens. Pour into sterilized jars and seal immediately. Store in a cool, dark place.

RHUBARB AND GINGER MINT PRESERVE

Ginger is a traditional flavouring for rhubarb jam, but in this recipe the flavour is boosted further by the addition of ginger mint, which is easily grown in the garden. The soft pink of the preserve is prettily set off by the fresh green flecks of the herb.

- 2 kg/4½ lb rhubarb
- 250 ml/8 fl oz/ 1 cup water
- juice of 1 lemon
- 5 cm/2 in piece fresh root ginger
- 1.5 kg/3 lb/6 cups sugar
- 115 g/4 oz preserved stem ginger, chopped
- 30–45 ml/2–3 tbsp very finely chopped ginger mint leaves

1 Wash and trim the rhubarb, cutting it into small pieces about 2.5 cm/1 in long. Place the rhubarb, water and lemon juice in a preserving pan and bring to the boil. Peel and bruise the piece of fresh root ginger and add it to the pan. Simmer, stirring frequently, until the rhubarb is soft. Remove the ginger.

2 Add the sugar and stir until it has dissolved. Bring the mixture to the boil and boil rapidly for 10–15 minutes, or until setting point is reached. With a metal slotted spoon, remove any scum from the surface of the jam. Add the stem ginger and ginger mint leaves. Pour into warmed, sterilized jars and seal.

DRIED APRICOT JAM

This is a jam which can be made at any time of year, so it is useful late in the winter when the jams and jellies you made during the previous summer are running low.

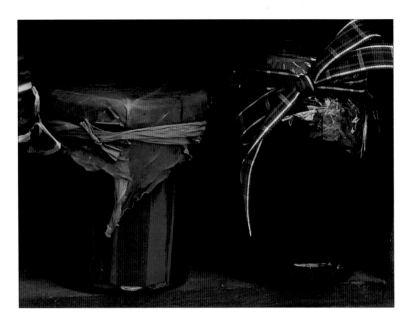

- 675 g/1½ lb dried apricots
- 900 ml/1½ pints/3¾ cups apple juice made with concentrate
- juice and rind of 2 lemons

- 675 g/1½ lb/3 cups sugar
- 50 g/2 oz blanched almonds, coarsely chopped

1 Soak the apricots in the apple juice overnight. Pour the soaked apricots and juice into a preserving pan and add the lemon juice and rind. Bring the mixture to the boil, lower the heat, then leave to simmer for 15–20 minutes, until the apricots are soft. Meanwhile, warm the sugar in a low oven (120°C/250°F/Gas ½).

2 Add the warmed sugar to the apricots and heat gently, stirring, until the sugar has dissolved completely. Increase the heat and boil until setting point is reached.

3 Stir in the chopped almonds and leave to stand for 15 minutes. Pour into warmed, sterilized jars and seal.

DAMSON JAM

If you are lucky enough to find a damson tree growing wild in the hedgerow, gather its deep purple fruits to make this richly flavoured jam.

- 1 kg/2¼ lb damson plums
- 1.4 litres/2¼ pints/6 cups water

- 1 kg/2¼ lb/4¼ cups sugar

1 Place the plums in a preserving pan, pour in the water and bring to the boil. Reduce the heat and simmer gently until the plums are soft. Meanwhile, warm the sugar in a low oven (120°C/250°F/Gas ½).

2 Stir in the warmed sugar and bring gently to the boil again, stirring until the sugar has dissolved and skimming off the damson stones as they rise to the surface (most can be removed this way).

3 Boil until setting point is reached, then leave to stand for 15 minutes. Pour the jam into warmed, sterilized jars and seal.

SCENTED GERANIUM LEAF JELLY

Scented geraniums, especially the rose-scented varieties, give a delicious perfume to clear apple jelly. Eat this with pork, ham or duck, or serve it on buttered scones or muffins.

- 1.5 kg/3¼ lb cooking apples, roughly chopped
- 1.75 litres/3 pints/7½ cups water
- juice of 2 large lemons

- about 20 large scented geranium (pelargonium) leaves, plus extra to decorate
- sugar (see method)

1 Put the apples in a large pan with the water, lemon juice and scented geranium leaves stripped from their stalks. Bring to the boil and simmer until the fruit is tender.

2 Strain the fruit and liquid through a jelly bag suspended over a large bowl and leave for at least 2 hours. Do not squeeze the bag, or the juice will be cloudy.

3 Measure the juice and pour it into the cleaned pan. Add 450 g/1 lb/ 2 cups sugar to each 600 ml/1 pint/2½ cups juice. Stir over a low heat to dissolve the sugar, then bring to the boil. Boil for about 10 minutes, until setting point is reached.

4 Pour the preserve into warmed, sterilized jars or glasses and place a washed scented geranium leaf on the surface of each before sealing with waxed paper circles and transparent paper covers.

CRANBERRY PRESERVE

As an alternative to traditional cranberry sauce to accompany your festive turkey, try this preserve, which is equally delicious spread on muffins or toast.

- 450 g/1 lb cranberries
- 1 kg/2¼ lb cooking apples, peeled, cored and chopped

- 350 ml/12 fl oz/1½ cups water
- 1.5 kg/3 lb/6 cups sugar

1 Put the cranberries and apples in a pan with the water, bring to the boil and simmer gently until the fruit is tender, stirring occasionally.

2 Add the sugar and stir over a low heat to dissolve it completely, then bring to the boil. Boil fast, stirring frequently, until setting point is reached. Pour into warmed, sterilized jars or glasses and seal.

CRAB-APPLE AND LAVENDER JELLY

This fragrant, clear jelly looks especially pretty with a sprig of fresh lavender suspended in the jar. You could use other fruits, such as apples, quince or rosehips.

- 900 g/2 lb crab-apples
- 1.75 litres/3 pints/7½ cups water
- lavender stems
- 900 g/2 lb/4 cups sugar

1 Cut the crab-apples into chunks and place in a preserving pan with the water and two stems of lavender. Bring to the boil and simmer gently, covered, for 1 hour, stirring occasionally. Strain the fruit and liquid through a jelly bag suspended over a large bowl and leave for several hours. Do not squeeze the bag, or the juice will be cloudy.

2 Discard the pulp and measure the juice. To each 600 ml/ 1 pint/2½ cups juice, add 450 g/1 lb/2 cups sugar and pour into a clean pan. Heat gently, stirring, until the sugar has dissolved, then boil rapidly for about 8–10 minutes, or until setting point is reached.

3 Remove the pan from the heat and use a slotted spoon to remove any froth from the surface. Pour into warmed, sterilized jars. Dip lavender stems quickly into boiling water and insert a stem into each jar. Seal with waxed paper circles and transparent paper covers.

ROSE PETAL JELLY

This subtle jelly is ideal for dainty afternoon teas with thin slices of bread and butter – it adds a real summer afternoon flavour to the bread.

- 600 ml/1 pint/2½ cups red or pink rose petals
- 450 ml/¾ pint/1¾ cups water
- 700 g/1 lb 9 oz/3 cups sugar
- 120 ml/4 fl oz/½ cup white grape juice
- 120 ml/4 fl oz/½ cup red grape juice
- 50 g/2 oz packet powdered fruit pectin
- 30 ml/2 tbsp rose water

1 Trim all the rose petals at the base to remove the white tips. Place the petals, water and 75 g/ 3 oz/⅓ cup sugar in a pan and bring to the boil. Reduce the heat and simmer for 5 minutes, remove from the heat, and leave overnight for the fragrance to infuse.

2 Strain the petals from the syrup and put it into a preserving pan. Add the grape juices and pectin. Boil hard for 1 minute. Add the rest of the sugar and stir well to dissolve. Boil the mixture hard for 1 minute more.

3 Remove from the heat to test for setting: it should make a soft jelly, not a thick jam. Return to the heat if necessary and test again until the jelly sets. Add the rose water. Ladle the jelly into sterilized glass jars, seal and label.

APPLE AND MINT JELLY

This jelly is a classic accompaniment to rich, roasted lamb, and it is also delicious served with garden peas.

- 900 g/2 lb cooking apples
- sugar (see method)
- 45 ml/3 tbsp chopped fresh mint

1 Chop the apples roughly and put them into a preserving pan. Add enough water to cover and simmer until the fruit is soft.

2 Strain through a jelly bag, allowing it to drip overnight. Do not squeeze the bag or the jelly will become cloudy.

3 Measure the amount of juice. To every 600 ml/1 pint/2½ cups of juice, add 500 g/ 1¼ lb/2¼ cups sugar. Place the juice and sugar in a large pan and heat gently to dissolve the sugar. Bring to the boil.

4 After about 10 minutes, test for setting by pouring about 5 ml/1 tsp into a saucer and leaving to cool slightly. If a wrinkle forms on the surface when pushed with a fingertip, the jelly will set. Leave to cool.

5 Stir in the mint and pour the jelly into warmed, sterilized jars. Seal the jars immediately and store in a cool, dark place for up to a year.

PRESERVED FRUITS AND VEGETABLES

To satisfy your hoarding instinct, try stocking your store cupboard with an interesting supply of bottled fruits and vegetables. Preserving whole fruits calls for unblemished specimens and very careful, gentle cooking, but a generous jar of spiced plums in brandy, or cherries in Kirsch, makes a magnificent gift and is just right for Christmas. Glacé fruits take a long time to make but the

results look and taste stunning, while home-made candied peel makes a lovely cake ingredient or decoration. For a special celebration, try crystallizing your own flowers.

Pickling fruit and vegetables allows you to enjoy them long after their growing season is over.

FRUITS IN LIQUEURS

Make these beautiful preserves when the fruits are in season and store them away to make luxurious Christmas gifts.
Choose from apricots, clementines, kumquats, physalis, cherries, raspberries, peaches, plums or seedless grapes and team them with
rum, brandy, Kirsch or Cointreau.

- 450 g/1 lb fresh fruit
- 225 g/8 oz/1 cup sugar
- 150 ml/¼ pint/ ⅔ cup liqueur or spirit

1 Wash the fruit, then prepare it. Halve and stone apricots, plums or peaches. Peel back and remove the husk from physalis, hull strawberries, and prick kumquats, cherries or grapes all over with a cocktail stick. Pare the rind and pith from clementines.

2 Place 115 g/4 oz/½ cup sugar and 300 ml/ ½ pint/1¼ cups water in a saucepan. Heat gently, stirring occasionally, until the sugar has dissolved. Bring to the boil. Add the fruit to the syrup and simmer for 1–2 minutes, until the fruit is just tender but still whole.

3 Remove the fruit and arrange neatly in warmed, sterilized jars. Add the remaining sugar to the syrup and stir until it has dissolved completely. Boil rapidly until the syrup reaches 107°C/225°F or the thread stage. Test by pressing a little syrup between two spoons: when pulled apart a thread should form.

4 Allow to cool, then measure the quantity of cooled syrup. Add an equal quantity of liqueur or spirit and mix together. Pour this mixture over the fruit in the jars until covered. Seal each jar with a screw or clip top, label and keep for up to 4 months.

CHERRIES IN EAU DE VIE

These cherries should be consumed with caution as they pack quite a punch. Serve them with chocolate torte or as a wicked garnish for a rice pudding.

- 450 g/1 lb ripe cherries
- 8 blanched almonds
- 90 ml/6 tbsp sugar
- 500 ml/17 fl oz/ 2¼ cups eau de vie

Wash and pit the cherries, then pack them with the almonds into a sterilized, wide-necked bottle. Spoon the sugar over the fruit, then cover with the eau de vie and seal securely. Store for a month before using the cherries, and shake the bottle every now and then to help dissolve the sugar.

SPICED POACHED PLUMS IN BRANDY

Bottling spiced fruit is a great way to preserve summer flavours for eating in winter. Serve these potent plums with whipped cream as a dessert.

- 600 ml/1 pint/ 2½ cups brandy
- 350 g/12 oz/ 1½ cups sugar
- 1 cinnamon stick
- 900 g/2 lb plums
- rind of 1 lemon, in a long strip

1 Put the brandy, sugar and cinnamon stick into a large pan and heat gently to dissolve the sugar. Add the plums and lemon rind and poach for 15 minutes, or until soft.

2 Remove the plums with a slotted spoon. Reduce the syrup by a third by rapid boiling. Strain it over the plums. Bottle the plums in large, sterilized jars. Seal tightly and store for up to 6 months in a cool, dark place.

CRANBERRY AND PORT SAUCE WITH LEMON THYME

Cranberry and port sauce is delicious served with roast turkey, but it also tastes very good with chicken, pork or ham. Lemon thyme really sets off its unique, tart flavour.

- 60 ml/4 tbsp port
- 60 ml/4 tbsp orange juice
- 115 g/4 oz/½ cup sugar
- 225 g /8 oz/1 cup cranberries
- 15 ml/1 tbsp finely grated orange rind
- 15 ml/1 tbsp very finely chopped lemon thyme

1 Pour the port and orange juice into a saucepan and add the sugar. Heat gently, stirring frequently, to dissolve the sugar.

2 Add the cranberries, bring the mixture to the boil and simmer for 5 minutes, stirring occasionally, until the cranberries are just tender and the skins begin to burst.

3 Remove the pan from the heat and mix in the grated orange rind and lemon thyme. Leave the sauce to cool, then pour into sterilized jars and seal.

GLACÉ FRUITS

These luxury sweetmeats are a traditional Christmas treat. You can save a fortune by making them at home, and though the whole process takes about a month, the result is well worth the effort. Choose one type of fruit or make a selection from cherries, plums, peaches, apricots, starfruit, pineapple, apples, oranges, lemons, limes and clementines.

- 450 g/1 lb fruit
- 1 kg/2¼ lb/ 4½ cups sugar
- 115 g/4 oz/½ cup powdered glucose

1 Carefully prepare the fruits. Stone cherries, plums, peaches and apricots. Peel and core pineapple and cut into cubes or rings. Peel, core and quarter apples, slice citrus fruits thinly. Prick cherries with a needle to allow the syrup to penetrate the skin.

2 Cook the fruit in batches if necessary. Place in the bottom of a saucepan, cover with water and simmer very gently until almost tender. Lift out the fruit with a slotted spoon and place in a shallow dish.

3 Measure 300 ml/½ pint/1¼ cups of the cooking liquid, adding water if necessary. Add 100 g/3½ oz/scant ½ cup sugar and the glucose. Heat gently, stirring, to dissolve. Bring to the boil and pour over the fruit to cover it. Leave overnight. Next day, drain the syrup into a pan and add 100 g/3½ oz/scant ½ cup sugar. Heat gently to dissolve, then bring to the boil. Pour over the fruit and leave overnight again.

4 Repeat for 5 more days, adding 100 g/3½ oz/scant ½ cup sugar each day. Drain off the syrup, dissolve 150 g/6 oz/¾ cup sugar in it and bring to the boil. Add the fruit and cook gently for 3 minutes. Return to the dish and leave for 2 days. Repeat. The syrup should look like runny honey. Leave the fruit in the syrup for at least 10 days, or up to 3 weeks.

5 Remove the fruit from the syrup and arrange on a wire rack over a tray. Dry in a warm place or in the oven at the lowest setting until the surface no longer feels sticky. If you wish, hold each fruit on a fork and plunge into boiling water, then roll in granulated sugar. Arrange the fruits in paper sweet cases and pack into boxes.

CANDIED FRUITS

Home-made candied fruit bears little or no resemblance in flavour or appearance to the packets of mixed peel available in the shops. It is so delicious that it can be eaten on its own as a sweetmeat as well as being a lovely addition to your cakes and puddings.

CANDIED PEEL RIBBONS

Make candied peel in the latter part of winter when the new season's citrus fruit arrives: it will keep all year round. The same process may be used to candy orange slices and larger pieces of citrus peel. To preserve the individual flavour of each fruit – lemons, limes and oranges – they should all be candied separately. Any syrup that is left over can be used in fruit salads or drizzled over a freshly baked sponge cake.

- 5 large oranges or 10 lemons or limes, unwaxed
- 675 g / 1½ lb / 3 cups sugar, plus extra for sprinkling

1 Halve the fruit, squeeze out the juice and reserve for another use. Discard the flesh of the fruit, but not the pith.

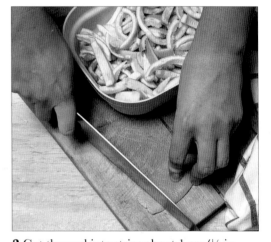

2 Cut the peel into strips about 1 cm / ½ in wide and place in a pan. Cover with boiling water and simmer for 5 minutes. Drain, then repeat four times, using fresh water each time to remove the peel's bitterness.

3 Put the sugar into a heavy-based saucepan, pour 250 ml / 8 fl oz / 1 cup water over it and heat gently, stirring, to dissolve. Add the peel and cook slowly, partially covered, for 30–40 minutes, or until soft. Leave to cool completely, then sprinkle with sugar.

CANDIED GINGER

Now that good quality fresh root ginger is easily available, it is practical to candy your own. It will keep indefinitely in an airtight jar.

- 350 g/12 oz fresh root ginger
- 225 g/8 oz/1 cup sugar

- caster (superfine) sugar, for coating

1 Place the ginger in a saucepan, cover with water and boil gently for about 15 minutes until tender. Drain thoroughly and peel when cold. Cut the ginger into 5 mm/¼ in slices.
2 In a heavy-based saucepan, dissolve the sugar in 120 ml/4 fl oz/½ cup water and cook, without stirring, over a low heat for about 15 minutes until the mixture becomes syrupy.
3 Add the ginger slices and continue to cook gently, shaking the pan occasionally to prevent the ginger sticking, until it has absorbed the syrup. Remove the cooked ginger slices, place them on a wire rack and leave to cool.
4 When cool, coat the slices with caster sugar and leave them spread out on greaseproof paper for 2–3 days to dry.

CRYSTALLIZED FLOWERS

❧

Crystallized flowers and petals make delicate, fragrant decorations for cakes and puddings. Pick fresh, perfect blooms for this purpose, making sure that they have not been sprayed with any sort of pesticide and are not growing near a busy road.

CRYSTALLIZED ROSES

You can crystallize individual petals, or use complete flower-heads to make a romantic cake decoration. Rinse and dry the petals carefully, then remove the white triangle at the base of each petal. When preparing whole blooms, leave a short piece of stem to hold them by.

- rose petals or flower-heads
- egg white
- icing (confectioner's) sugar

1 Each petal or bloom must be completely covered with a thin, even layer of lightly beaten egg white. Use a paintbrush that reaches right into the flower and don't forget to coat the backs of the petals. Work quickly.

2 Sprinkle sifted icing (confectioner's) sugar evenly over the petals and shake off the excess, to avoid a patchy effect. A regular, even coating will preserve the roses most successfully.

3 Leave the petals or blooms to dry on a wire rack. Stored between layers of tissue paper, the petals will keep for about a week in a cool, dry place – do not put them in the fridge.

CRYSTALLIZED LAVENDER

This perfumed decorative garnish for sweets and puddings makes a refreshing alternative to crystallized violets. It is best to take the individual florets off the rather unpalatable stems. While well-spaced florets are easy to remove after crystallizing, you may find it easier to separate the flowers of the tightly packed varieties, such as 'Hidcote', before crystallizing them.

- fresh lavender heads
- egg white
- caster (superfine) sugar

1 Rinse and dry the lavender heads, and remove the florets from the stems if you wish.

2 Using tweezers if necessary, dip each flower-head or floret first into lightly whisked egg white, then into caster sugar. Leave to dry on sheets of greaseproof paper.
3 When they are completely dried out, you can store them between layers of greaseproof paper in an airtight container for up to 3 months.

Bottled Vegetables

❧

Now that fresh vegetables are freely available all year round, we no longer need to rely on bottled vegetables in the way previous generations did, but they are still an excellent store cupboard standby. With the addition of herbs and spices they can be turned from a staple to a luxury item.

BOTTLED CHERRY TOMATOES

Cherry tomatoes bottled in their own juices with garlic and basil are sweetly delicious and a perfect accompaniment to thick slices of country ham.

- 1 kg/2¼ lb cherry tomatoes
- 5 ml/1 tsp salt per 1 litre/1¾ pint/ 4 cup jar
- 5 ml/1 tsp sugar

- per 1 litre/ 1¾ pint/4 cup jar
- fresh basil
- 5 garlic cloves per 1 litre/1¾ pint/ 4 cup jar

1 Prick the skins of the tomatoes with a toothpick and place them in clean, dry jars.

2 Sprinkle salt and sugar over the layers of tomatoes as you go. Fill the jars to within 2 cm/¾ in of the top.

3 Tuck the basil and garlic among the tomatoes. Rest the lids on the jars but do not seal. Stand them on a baking tray lined with newspaper in a low oven (120°C/ 250°F/ Gas ½). When the juice is simmering, remove the jars from the oven and seal immediately.

PICKLED BEETROOT

The beetroots for this pickle can be baked or boiled – baking will make them taste richer and earthier. However, if you prefer to boil them, cook them in their skins to retain their colour and leave to cool in the cooking liquid before gently rubbing off the skins.

- 450 g/1 lb beetroot, cooked
- 1 large onion, sliced
- 300 ml/½ pint/ 1¼ cups cider vinegar

- 50 g/2 oz/¼ cup sugar
- few strips fresh horseradish (optional)

1 Slice the beetroot and pack it into a jar, layering it with the sliced onion. Pour the vinegar and 150 ml/¼ pint/⅔ cup water into a saucepan.
2 Add the sugar and horseradish, if using, and bring to the boil. Pour the liquid over the beetroot and seal the jar.
3 Store in a cool place and use within a month, or longer if kept in the fridge.

PICKLED RED CABBAGE

This pickle is good served with bread and cheese or with cold duck or goose.

- 675 g/1½ lb red cabbage, shredded
- 1 large Spanish onion, sliced
- 15 ml/1 tbsp sea salt
- 600 ml/1 pint/ 2½ cups red wine vinegar
- 75 g/3 oz/⅓ cup brown sugar
- 15 ml/1 tbsp coriander seeds
- 3 cloves
- 2.5 cm/1 in piece fresh root ginger
- 1 star anise
- 2 bay leaves
- 2 eating apples

1 Mix the cabbage and onion thoroughly with the salt, place in a colander and allow to drain overnight.

2 Rinse and rub the vegetables dry with a clean cloth. Pour the vinegar into a saucepan, add the sugar, spices and bay leaves. Bring to the boil, then allow to cool.

3 Core and coarsely chop the apples and layer them with the cabbage and onions in clean, dry preserving jars. Pour on the cooled, spiced vinegar (strain out the spices if you prefer a milder pickle), seal and store for a week before eating. Pickled cabbage is at its best eaten within 2 months.

PRESERVED MUSHROOMS

Mushrooms are perfect for preserving and retain their flavour and succulence. If you are a wild-mushroom picker, use these recipes and stock your pantry with enough for the year.

PICKLED MUSHROOMS

It is a good idea to dress pickled mushrooms with olive oil when serving, to temper the sharpness of the vinegar. Serve these as an appetizer or as part of a buffet lunch.

- 250 ml/8 fl oz/1 cup white wine vinegar
- 150 ml/¼ pint/⅔ cup water
- 5 ml/1 tsp salt
- 1 red chilli

- 10 ml/2 tsp coriander seeds
- 10 ml/2 tsp Szechuan pepper or anise-pepper
- 250 g/9 oz shiitake mushrooms, halved if large

1 Bring the wine vinegar and water to a simmer in a saucepan. Add the salt, chilli, coriander, pepper and mushrooms and cook for 10 minutes.

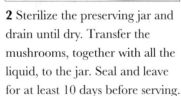

2 Sterilize the preserving jar and drain until dry. Transfer the mushrooms, together with all the liquid, to the jar. Seal and leave for at least 10 days before serving.

SPICED MUSHROOMS IN VODKA

Winter chanterelles and oyster mushrooms combine with caraway seeds, lemon and chilli to make this unusual infusion which can be served as a warming apéritif.

- 75 g/3 oz winter chanterelles and oyster mushrooms
- 5 ml/1 tsp caraway seeds

- 1 lemon
- 1 red chilli
- 350 ml/12 fl oz/1½ cups vodka

1 Place the cleaned mushrooms, caraway seeds, lemon and chilli in a clean preserving jar or bottle.

2 Add the vodka and leave for 2–3 weeks, until the mushrooms no longer float. Chill before serving.

FLAVOURED CONDIMENTS

Flavouring oils, vinegars, mustards and butters is easy and satisfying and will transform all your cooking and inspire new dishes.  Use these indispensable condiments to form the basis of new dressings and sauces and to complement plain grilled fish, meat and vegetables. Drizzle spicy chilli oil over a pizza, or sprinkle a dash of raspberry vinegar over a fruit salad. Packed into pretty bottles or  pots, all these suggestions make perfect gifts for keen cooks. If you can, tuck a fresh sprig of the flavouring ingredient into the oil or vinegar: it will look wonderful as well as identifying the flavour.

FLAVOURED VINEGARS

Use good quality, mellow wine vinegar as the basis for these fruit and herb variations. All flavoured vinegars are best used within three months.

RASPBERRY VINEGAR

Raspberry vinegar gives a delicious depth of flavour to salad dressings and, if used sparingly, will enhance the flavour of fruit such as strawberries and nectarines that are not quite ripe.

- 600 ml/1 pint/ 2½ cups red wine vinegar
- 15 ml/1 tbsp. pickling spice
- 450 g/1 lb raspberries, fresh or frozen
- 2 sprigs fresh lemon thyme

2 Pour the hot vinegar mixture over the raspberries in a bowl and then add the sprig of lemon thyme.

1 Pour the vinegar into a saucepan, add the pickling spice and heat gently for 5 minutes.

3 Cover and leave the mixture to infuse for 2 days in a cool, dark place, stirring occasionally. Strain the liquid to remove the thyme and raspberries, pour into a clean, dry bottle and seal with a cork.

LEMON AND LIME VINEGAR

Citrus-flavoured vinegar is wonderful for piquant sauces such as hollandaise.

- 600 ml/1 pint/ 2½ cups white wine vinegar
- rind of 1 lime
- rind of 1 lemon

Bring the vinegar to the boil in a saucepan, then pour it over the lime and lemon rind in a bowl. Cover and leave to infuse for 3 days. Strain and pour it into a clean, dry bottle, adding strips of fresh rind for colour.

ROSEMARY OR TARRAGON VINEGAR

Herb vinegars are excellent for adding flavour to dressings and sauces.

- 600 ml/1 pint/ 2½ cups white wine or cider vinegar
- 90 ml/6 tbsp
- chopped fresh rosemary or tarragon, plus some whole sprigs

Bring the vinegar to the boil in a saucepan, then pour it over the herb in a bowl. Cover and leave to infuse for 3 days. Strain and pour it into a clean, dry bottle, adding a sprig of rosemary or tarragon for decoration.

FLAVOURED OILS

A selection of flavoured oils will bring the taste of summer to your cooking. All flavoured oils are best used within three months.

GARLIC OIL

This delicious oil can be used in salad dressings and to brush on fish, meat and vegetables whenever you want a gentle garlic flavour. Hang a garlic clove around the neck of the bottle to act as an identifying label.

- 25 large, plump garlic cloves
- 900 ml/1½ pints/
- 3¾ cups cold-pressed virgin olive oil

2 Add the garlic cloves and poach them for approximately 25 minutes, until they are tender and transparent.

1 Peel the garlic cloves. Pour the olive oil into a saucepan and heat to a gentle simmer.

3 Leave in the saucepan until cool, then strain the garlic from the oil and reserve. Pour the oil into a clean bottle, seal and use within 3 months. Use the garlic as a relish, or spread on toast as a starter.

CHILLI OIL

As well as drizzling this fiery oil over pizzas, you can use it when stir-frying or grilling vegetables. For a more robust flavour, add garlic, thyme and peppercorns to the oil.

- 500 ml/17 fl oz/ 2¼ cups virgin olive oil
- 1 small fresh green chilli
- a few small, fresh red chillies

1 Fill a clean, dry bottle with the olive oil. Slice the green chilli crossways into thin rings and add them with the whole red chillies to the oil.
2 Cork tightly and leave to infuse for 10–14 days. Shake the bottle occasionally during this time.

SAFFRON OIL

Saffron has never been surpassed as a flavouring. By weight it is certainly among the most expensive of spices, but a little saffron goes a long way, especially when you use it to infuse an oil with its delicate flavour and then brush the oil on to grilled fish.

- large pinch saffron strands
- 250 ml/8 fl oz/

1 cup olive oil or pure sunflower oil

1 Put the saffron strands into a clean, dry bottle. Fill the bottle with oil and seal with a cork.
2 Leave to infuse for 2 weeks, gently shaking the bottle daily, before using.

ROSE PETAL VINEGAR

This delicately scented vinegar can be used in a dressing for summer salads, and it is also effective as a cool compress to ease a nagging headache.

- 300 ml/½ pint/1¼ cups white wine vinegar
- scented red rose petals

1 Pull the rose petals from the flower-heads. Scald the vinegar by heating it to just below boiling point, then allow to cool.

2 Snip away the bitter white part at the base of each petal. Prepare enough petals to fill a cup and put into a glass jar or bottle.

3 Add the cooled vinegar, cover very tightly with a screw top or cork, and leave on a sunny windowsill for at least 3 weeks.

FLAVOURED MUSTARDS

HONEY MUSTARD

Honey mustard is richly flavoured and is delicious in sauces and salad dressings and for basting grilled or roasted meat.

- 225 g/8 oz/2 cups mustard seeds
- 15 ml/1 tbsp ground cinnamon
- 2.5 ml/½ tsp ground ginger
- 300 ml/½ pint/ 1¼ cups white wine vinegar
- 90 ml/6 tbsp dark runny honey

1 Mix the mustard seeds with the spices, pour on the vinegar and then leave to soak overnight.
2 Place the mixture in a mortar and pound until you have made a paste, all the while gradually adding the honey.
3 The finished mustard should resemble a stiff paste: add extra vinegar if necessary. Store in sterilized jars in the fridge. Use within 4 weeks.

HORSERADISH MUSTARD

An excellent accompaniment to cold meats, smoked fish or cheese.

- 25 g/1 oz/¼ cup mustard seeds
- 115 g/4 oz/1 cup mustard powder
- 115 g/4 oz/½ cup sugar
- 120 ml/4 fl oz/½ cup white
- wine or cider vinegar
- 50 ml/2 fl oz/¼ cup olive oil
- 5 ml/1 tsp lemon juice
- 30 ml/2 tbsp horseradish sauce

1 Place the mustard seeds in a bowl and pour 250 ml/8 fl oz/1 cup boiling water over them. Leave for 1 hour. Drain and place in the bowl of a blender with the remaining ingredients.
2 Blend the mixture into a smooth paste and then spoon it into sterilized jars. Store in the fridge and use within 3 months.

FLAVOURED BUTTERS

Butter blended with herbs or other flavourings is delicious simply spread on fresh, crusty bread or as a garnish for grilled fish, meat or vegetables.

ROASTED PEPPER BUTTER

Roasting red peppers transforms their flavour; when combined with butter, they make a rich, sweet spread that is ideal for picnics and barbecues.

• 1 small red pepper	butter at room
• 15 ml/1 tbsp	temperature
lemon juice	• olive oil
• 115 g/4 oz/½ cup	• salt and pepper

1 Cut the pepper in half and grill, turning regularly, until the skin is blackened. Remove from the heat and wrap in foil for 10–15 minutes; this helps to loosen the skin.

2 Peel the pepper, remove the stalk and pips and slice thinly. Place the pepper in the bowl of a food processor or a mortar and blend to a paste with the lemon juice and a pinch of salt.

3 Add the butter and seasoning and mix thoroughly. For a smooth paste, blend in a little olive oil, a teaspoon at a time, until the ingredients hold together.

HERB BUTTER

Most herbs can be blended with butter and used to finish cooked dishes. Try mint butter on peas, dill butter on fish, or parsley butter on potatoes. These butters are also delicious when spread on cheese scones, added to stews for a velvety finish, or used as a base for sauces.

• 175 g/6 oz/¾ cup	• 90 ml/6 tbsp
butter at room	chopped fresh herbs
temperature	• salt and pepper

1 Blend the butter with the herbs and seasoning using a mortar and pestle or food processor.
2 Transfer to ramekins and chill if it is for immediate use.
3 Alternatively, spoon the butter on to greaseproof paper, roll up into a log shape and freeze for a couple of hours.
4 Unroll, cut into slices and place in a plastic bag in the freezer, ready for use. Use within 2 months for the best flavour.

LIME BUTTER

When topped with lime butter, a dish of simple grilled fish is given a wonderfully exotic flavour.

- finely grated rind of 2 limes plus juice of 1 lime
- 115 g/4 oz/½ cup
- butter at room temperature
- salt and pepper

Blend all the ingredients using a food processor or a mortar and pestle, and chill for at least 2 hours before using.

GARLIC BUTTER

The most popular of flavoured butters, garlic butter can be used to enliven almost any dish and is the essential ingredient for garlic bread.

- 4 garlic cloves
- 5 ml/1 tsp sea salt
- 15 ml/1 tbsp chopped parsley
- 115 g/4 oz/½ cup
- butter at room temperature
- 15 ml/1 tbsp lemon juice
- salt and pepper

1 Finely chop the garlic and blend to a paste with the sea salt using a mortar and pestle.
2 Blend the garlic paste with the parsley, then beat into the butter with the lemon juice and seasoning. Alternatively, you could mix all the ingredients in a food processor.
3 Transfer the garlic butter to ramekins and chill, or freeze as for Herb Butter.

ANCHOVY BUTTER

Spread on fingers of wholemeal toast, this is a sublime tea-time treat.

- 12 anchovy fillets, soaked in milk for 1 hour
- 115 g/4 oz/½ cup butter at room
- temperature
- juice of 1 lemon
- cayenne pepper
- black pepper
- olive oil

1 Drain the anchovy fillets and, using a mortar and pestle, pound to a paste.
2 Mix with the butter. Season with the lemon juice, cayenne pepper and black pepper, and to give the butter a smooth texture, slowly add a small quantity of olive oil.
3 Finally, pack the butter into a small jar or ramekins. Refrigerate, and use within 10 days, or freeze for future use.

YOGURT CHEESE IN OLIVE OIL

Sheep's milk is widely used in cheese-making in the Eastern Mediterranean, particularly in Greece where sheep's yogurt is hung in cheesecloth to drain off the whey before patting into balls of soft cheese. Here, it's bottled in olive oil with chilli and herbs to make an appetizing and beautiful gift.

- 800 g/1¾ lb sheep's yogurt
- 2.5 ml/½ tsp salt
- 10 ml/2 tsp crushed dried chillies or chilli powder
- 15 ml/1 tbsp chopped fresh rosemary
- 15 ml/1 tbsp chopped fresh thyme or oregano
- 300 ml/½ pint/ 1¼ cups olive oil, flavoured with garlic

1 Sterilize a 30 cm/12 in square of cheesecloth by steeping it in boiling water. Drain and lay over a large plate. Mix the yogurt with the salt and tip into the centre of the cheesecloth. Bring up the sides and tie firmly with string.

2 Hang the bag in a position where you can place a bowl underneath to catch the whey (from a kitchen cupboard handle, for instance). Leave for 2–3 days, until it stops dripping.

3 Mix together the chilli and herbs. Take teaspoonfuls of the cheese and roll into balls between your hands. Lower into sterilized jars, sprinkling each layer with the herb mixture.

4 Pour the oil over the cheeses until they are completely covered. Store the jars in the fridge for up to 3 weeks. Serve the cheese with lightly toasted bread drizzled with the flavoured oil.

INDEX